Alexander Graham Bell

by Victoria Sherrow
illustrations by Elaine Verstraete

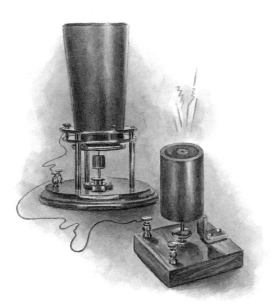

Carolrhoda Books, Inc. / Minneapolis

Text copyright © 2001 by Victoria Sherrow
Illustrations copyright © 2001 by Elaine Verstraete

This book is available in two editions:
Library binding by Carolrhoda Books, Inc., a division of Lerner Publishing Group
Soft cover by First Avenue Editions, an imprint of Lerner Publishing Group
241 First Avenue North
Minneapolis, MN 55401 U.S.A.

Website address: www.lernerbooks.com

Library of Congress Cataloging-in-Publication Data

Sherrow, Victoria.
    Alexander Graham Bell / by Victoria Sherrow ; illustrations by Elaine Verstraete.
        p.   cm. — (On my own biography)
    ISBN 1–57505–460–4 (lib. bdg. : alk. paper)
    ISBN 1–57505–533–3 (pbk. : alk. paper)
    1. Bell, Alexander Graham, 1847–1922—Juvenile literature. 2. Inventors—
United States—Biography. [1. Bell, Alexander Graham, 1847–1922. 2. Inventors.]
I. Verstraete, Elaine, ill. II. Title. III. Series.
TK140.B37 S47 2001
621.385′092—dc21   2001000727

Manufactured in the United States of America
1 2 3 4 5 6 – JR – 06 05 04 03 02 01

To my husband, Peter, with much love
　　　　　　　　　　　　—V. S.

For Francis, whose friendship I value
　　　　　　　　　　　　—E. V.

Edinburgh, Scotland
1857

Melville and Edward Bell sat
on the carpet, waiting.
Where was Aleck?
Their brother had promised them
a surprise.

Finally, Aleck burst in with the family dog.

He opened the dog's jaws.

Then he pressed the sides of his throat.

The dog made noises

that sounded like words.

Aleck explained.

He was teaching the dog to talk!

He opened the dog's mouth again.

He pressed his throat in different ways.

His brothers tried to help.

Aleck patted the dog's head.

The dog's "words" might not be very clear.

But he was making new sounds.

And he seemed to enjoy learning.

Aleck and his brothers loved new projects.

The whole Bell family

had a special interest in speech.

Aleck's father and grandfather

were famous speech teachers.

Aleck's father found ways
to help deaf people learn new things.
Deaf people cannot hear spoken words.
They cannot learn to speak the same way
hearing people do.
In those days, many people who were
born deaf were not taught to read or write.
They were cut off from the speaking world.
Aleck's mother, Eliza Bell,
was a talented artist and pianist.
Eliza had begun to lose her hearing.
But she taught her sons to read and write.
She taught them to love art and music.

9

Aleck learned to play the piano.

He planned to become a musician.

Aleck also spent hours outdoors.

He loved exploring nature.

He loved collecting leaves.

Aleck read about the plants he found.

Sometimes, he stared at the sky.

He wondered how birds could fly.

Aleck was full of questions.

School Days

1858

Both Aleck and his grandfather
were named Alexander Bell.
Aleck's father was Alexander Melville Bell.
When Aleck was 11 years old,
he gave himself a middle name.
He chose the name of a family friend.
Now he was Alexander Graham Bell.
At school, Aleck liked science and music.
But he did poorly
in Latin, math, and geography.
During these lessons,
his mind would wander.

Aleck's parents sent him to London
to spend a year with his grandfather.
By day, Aleck went to school.
At night, he studied hard
in his grandfather's library.
Sometimes they read plays together.
Aleck became a serious student.

He missed his family.
But he enjoyed exploring London.
He and Grandfather Bell went to parks,
concerts, museums, and theaters.
He also took piano lessons.
Aleck was 16 years old
when he returned home.
He was taller and more grown-up.
He said his year in London
turned him "into a man."

The Science of Sound

In 1863, Aleck went to a new school.

Life was busier than ever.

He taught music and public speaking

to younger boys.

He worked on inventions, too.

He and Melville made a "talking machine"

shaped like a human head.

It had a tin "throat"
and rubber "cheeks" and "lips."
Inside the throat was a rubber "windpipe."
They pumped air through the windpipe
to make the machine speak.
The boys hid the machine in a closet.
People who heard it thought a baby
was crying out "Ma-ma!"

Aleck also helped his father.

Professor Bell had made a "sound alphabet."

He called it Visible Speech.

There were pictures for every letter

from A to Z.

The pictures showed how to move the
mouth to make each sound.
They would show deaf people how to talk.
The three boys helped their father
teach people how to use Visible Speech.

In 1864, Aleck went to college.

He loved his science classes.

He learned more and more about speech.

Aleck also spent hours studying sound.

He studied the way a piano works.

Its strings vibrated back and forth.

The vibrations made sounds.

Aleck also worked with steel tuning forks.

These metal forks vibrated, too.

They made different sounds, depending on how fast they vibrated in the air.

Fast vibrations made high sounds.

Slow vibrations made lower sounds.

After college, Aleck went back to London.

He taught at a school for deaf children.

Aleck knew that he wanted to spend his life helping deaf people.

By this time, his own mother was deaf.

A New Home

Tragedy struck in 1867.

Edward Bell died from a lung disease.

Just three years later, Melville died

from the same disease.

Then Aleck became ill, too.

The Bells were sad and worried.

They left Scotland for a farmhouse

in southern Canada.

Hopefully Aleck would get well

in the clean country air.

For eight months, Aleck rested.

Sometimes he walked in the garden.

Often he lay in the hammock, thinking.

He thought about the things he might invent.

Aleck was excited about the telegraph.

Samuel Morse had invented it
in the 1830s.

Written messages could travel
long distances on telegraph wires.

People tapped out messages.

They used a code Morse had created.

The messages arrived in minutes.

But a telegraph could send
only one message at a time.

Aleck wanted to make a new kind
of telegraph.

It would carry more than one message
at once.

It would carry them on the same wire.

Boston, Massachusetts

1871

In less than a year,
Aleck felt well enough to work.
A school for deaf children had opened
in Boston.
The head of the school wanted Aleck
to teach there.
Aleck wanted to use Visible Speech
to help more people.

The students and teachers liked
24-year-old Aleck Bell.
Aleck gave private lessons, too.
His first student was five-year-old
George Sanders.
George had been born deaf.
Aleck used Visible Speech.
He taught George to speak.

Aleck also taught a young woman
named Mabel Hubbard.
Mabel had lost her hearing at age four.
But she had learned to read and write
as a child.
She could also read lips.
Mabel watched people's lips move
to find out what they were saying.
She had learned to talk, too.
Mabel's father asked Aleck to help her
speak more clearly.

Aleck liked to visit the Hubbards.

Mr. Hubbard wanted to hear

about Aleck's inventions.

Hubbard was a wealthy lawyer.

He worked hard to improve schools

for deaf children.

He wanted more children
to have fine teachers like Mabel's.
Around the United States,
people heard about Aleck's work.
He visited different cities
to talk about Visible Speech.

An Inventive Team

Aleck still made time to work on
his new telegraph.
But he faced several problems.
He did not have money to buy supplies
for his project.
Mr. Sanders and Mr. Hubbard agreed
to help him.

Aleck had good ideas
about how to make things.
But he was not so good
at putting them together.
He paid men at a machine shop.
They would build the things he needed.
Aleck thought Thomas Watson
was the best mechanic in the shop.
The two men decided to work together.

Aleck and Watson worked at night

in the machine-shop attic.

Some nights, they did not sleep.

Mabel Hubbard joked about

Aleck's late nights working in the shop.

One day she drew a picture of him

with an owl's head!

Owls stayed awake at night, too.

By this time, Aleck and Mabel were in love.

Aleck hoped to marry Mabel.

Aleck kept working on the telegraph.

But he also had a new idea.

Aleck wanted to make a machine
that let people *talk* over wires.
He knew that air changes
when sounds move through it.
Vibrations make waves of sound in the air.
Maybe sound waves could also change
an electrical current.
If they could,
spoken words could be sent over a wire.

Aleck and Watson began to work
on a talking machine, too.
For months, they tried connecting wires
in different ways.
They built new kinds of transmitters.
Transmitters send a message.
They tried different receivers.
Receivers receive messages.
Nothing worked.

Exciting Sounds
June 2, 1875

One evening, Aleck and Watson
were working in the shop.
Watson was working on the transmitter
in one room.
Aleck was working on the receiver
in another.
Suddenly, Aleck heard a weak musical noise.
He ran toward Watson.

"What did you do,
Mr. Watson?" he asked.
"Don't change a thing.
I just heard a different
sound come through."
Watson said the transmitter had jammed.
He had tried to fix it.
He had moved the part that was stuck,
and a "twang" sound came over the wire.

Aleck and Watson tried sending the sound
over and over again.

It worked.

Quickly, Aleck drew a picture.

It showed his new design
for the talking machine.

Now he *knew* it was possible
for voices to travel on wires.

Aleck and Watson decided to spend
all their time on the talking machine.

Aleck stopped teaching for a while.

The two men worked harder than ever.

"I Heard Every Word!"
March 10, 1876

Aleck and Watson were hard at work.

Watson was downstairs

working on a receiver.

Aleck was upstairs.

He was working with the transmitter.

A pile of tools, wires, and battery acid
surrounded him.

Suddenly, Aleck spilled some acid.

The acid burned.

Aleck cried out, "Mr. Watson, come here!
I want to see you."

He forgot that Watson was too far away
to hear him.

To Aleck's surprise,
Watson came running upstairs.
He burst into the room.
"Mr. Bell, I heard you!" he said.
"I heard every word!"
Aleck forgot all about his burns.
He and Watson spent the night
talking on their machine.

The talking machine was finally a reality.
Aleck called it a "telephone."
Since his childhood, Alexander Graham Bell
had studied speech and sound.
He helped to build bridges
between deaf people and hearing people.
And his new telephone would bring
people together in new and exciting ways.

Afterword

Aleck took his new "talking machine" to a fair in Philadelphia in June 1876. Aleck won first prize for his invention. But no company wanted to make it and sell it. People called the telephone an "interesting toy." They said it was not really useful.

Mr. Hubbard and Mr. Sanders helped Aleck create the Bell Telephone Company. More Americans started buying telephones.

Aleck married Mabel Hubbard in 1877. The Bell family grew to include two daughters, Elsie and Daisy. They lived in Washington, D.C., and spent their summers in Canada. Mabel Bell often had trouble getting her "night owl" to sleep when he was working hard on an idea.

Aleck never ran out of ideas. He made an instrument to help doctors find metal objects in the human body. He worked on ways to change seawater into drinking water. He studied flight and made hundreds of kites and gliders. He said that humans would fly someday. People laughed at this idea. Aleck reminded them that people had laughed about his telephone, too.

Aleck became one of the most famous people in the world. Yet he always said his most important job was "teacher of the deaf." He helped many people. One of them was Helen Keller. An illness had left her blind and deaf at age one. Aleck found her a talented teacher named Anne Sullivan. Helen learned to read, write, and speak. She called Aleck a good friend.

In 1892, Aleck makes the first telephone call from New York to Chicago.

In 1915, Aleck made the first phone call across the United States. From New York, he called Thomas Watson in San Francisco. Smiling, Aleck said, "Mr. Watson, come here. I want to see you." Watson laughed. He said, "I'd like to Mr. Bell, but it might take me a while to get there."

Alexander Graham Bell died in 1922 at his home in Nova Scotia, Canada. That day, every telephone in the United States stayed silent for one minute in his honor.

Important Dates

March 3, 1847—Alexander Bell was born in Edinburgh, Scotland.

1862–63—Spent a year in London with his grandfather.

1864—Attended the University of Edinburgh.

1868—Taught speech at a school for deaf children; attended University College in London.

1870—Emigrated to Canada with his parents and sister-in-law, Carrie Bell.

1871—Moved to Boston; taught at the Boston School for Deaf Mutes.

1873—Appointed Professor of Vocal Physiology at Boston University; began teaching Mabel Hubbard.

1874—First thought of the idea for the telephone; met Thomas Watson.

March 10, 1876—Spoke the first words ever heard over the telephone.

June 25, 1876—Demonstrated the telephone at the Centennial Exhibition in Philadelphia.

July 11, 1877—Married Mabel Hubbard.

1878—Demonstrated the telephone for England's Queen Victoria.

1887—Met six-year-old blind and deaf Helen Keller.

1892—Opened long-distance telephone service between New York and Chicago.

August 2, 1922—Died and was buried in Nova Scotia.